# E·Z Bock's Best

*Volume IV*

## CONTENTS

# Hotel sur la Mar
# Cabo San Lucas, Mexico

January, 2004

Dear Fred Bock Music Company:

It's not often that I'm the one writing a letter requesting something. Usually it's the other way around. But, I've been patiently waiting for all these years, and, well, so far you haven't done it. So, I'm going to break from tradition and ask: When are you ever going to get around to releasing a Christmas volume of E Z Bock's Best?

You've already done three (which I've enjoyed immensely, I might add). They're all full of great arrangements of hymns and gospel songs and even a couple of Christmas Carols (thanks). I've played through each one about a thousand times. Great stuff! However, Christmas is its own special time of year, and it deserves its own book. No?

After a couple of years of giving Bock's Best #3 to countless pianists around the world, I thought I would try to play some of the arrangements. You know, my fingers just don't do what Fred seemed to be able to make his do. (Of course, he couldn't fit down a chimney, so I guess we're even.) That's why I was so pleased to see you start to publish the EZ Bock's Best series. There are many of us out here who simply can't play all those notes. Now, all you need to do is add a Christmas book to the line.

In case you need some help picking titles, I've always loved "O Come, O Come Emmanuel" and "Away in the Manger." You'd absolutely have to include "Silent Night." Oh, and don't forget to do "Mary, Did You Know?". I love that song. (Since I first heard that song, Buddy Green and Mark Lowry have been on my permanent "Nice" list.) I'm sure that you can come up with some other titles to create one book. I just gave you four. See, you're 40% done and you haven't even finished reading my letter!

Well, I've done it. It's up to you folks, now. Tell Lloyd Larson that he does a great job on these adaptations. And, you can add that if he gets a Christmas book done by this year, they'll be something extra special under the tree for him this December.

Merry Christmas to all, and to all a Good Night!

Kris

Kris Kringle

**Lloyd Larson Music**

**Minneapolis, Minnesota**

May, 2004

Dear Mr. Kringle:

The Fred Bock Music staff forwarded your letter to me about the possibility of doing a Christmas volume in the *EZ Bock's Best* series. It is truly an intriguing idea . . . but, of course, you are an "idea" guy, right? So I guess I shouldn't be surprised!

By the way, for many years I have been under the impression that you were immersed in Christmas preparation on-site at the North Pole virtually year-round. However, it has become clear, based on your letterhead, that your management skills have enabled you to head south for at least part of the off-season and direct operations from a distance. I'm impressed! It also sounds like you continue to keep your piano skills sharp, which I am certainly pleased to hear. Some daily scales and arpeggios will keep you playing for years (or in your case, decades or centuries!) to come.

Back to your idea . . . I decided to take you and the Fred Bock Music staff up on the suggestion to compile a Christmas collection in this series. As in the earlier three books, these are all Fred's arrangements. As you well know, his arrangements are never naughty, but always nice! However, as you correctly alluded to in your letter, they can sometimes be a little challenging for rusty or lesser-experienced pianists (not to mention those with slightly frostbitten fingers!). These arrangements are very user-friendly. They will not make you cry or pout . . . and I'm telling you why: you never find more than three notes played at one time in either hand; you never find octaves; you never find 16$^{th}$ notes. Yet, they are still Fred's distinctive settings of Christmas favorites done with his harmonies and rhythms. You will be humming these tunes when you are sleeping and when you are awake; maybe even when you are bad or good . . . though I'm not implying anything about YOU in that statement!

I've included all of your requested carols in this collection along with a few of my favorites. These will work very nicely in Christmas gatherings at church or parties or even times around the family piano. When you are making your list and checking it twice, you might consider including this book on the gift-list for the many good pianists you will visit later this year. I think you and they will enjoy it this Christmas and for many more to come.

Well, thanks for providing a good idea for celebrating Christmas. And thanks for promising something extra special under my tree this year. If you need any ideas in that regard, just let me know!

Sincerely,

Lloyd Larson

Lloyd Larson

# The Bock's Best Series of Outstanding Piano Arrangements of Hymns and Gospel Songs by Fred Bock

**Original Series by Fred Bock**

BG0557 Bock's Best Vol I
BG0572 Bock's Best Vol II
BG0679 Bock's Best Vol III
BG0880 Bock's Best Vol IV
BG0941 Bock's Best Vol V

**The E•Z Editions**

*adapted by Lloyd Larson*

BG0991 E•Z Bock's Best Vol I
BGK1007 E•Z Bock's Best Vol II
BGK1012 E•Z Bock's Best Vol III
BGK1026 E•Z Bock's Best Vol IV

**The Fred Bock Memorial Collection**

*Piano Solos in Celebration of the Life of Fred Bock Written by His Friends,*

Stephen Nielson, Kurt Kaiser, Ken Medema, Bob Krogstad, Paul Johnson, Dwight Elrich, Jan Sanborn, Mark Hayes, William Phemister, Dick Bolks, Ted Cornell, Michele Murray, Ovid Young and Don Wyrtzen.

BG0967 Bock's Best Friends

Fred Bock Music Company

All are available at your favorite music store.

# O COME, O COME, EMMANUEL

PLAINSONG
*Arranged by* FRED BOCK
*Adapted by* LLOYD LARSON

Strongly
Tenderly

39
43
f
47
50
dim. poco a poco
54
pp
pp
pp
pp
pp

# HE IS BORN, THE DIVINE CHRIST CHILD

FRENCH CAROL
*Arranged by* FRED BOCK
*Adapted by* LLOYD LARSON

21
f
25
mf
29
mp
33
37
f

41
45
49
Strongly
mp
f
53
simile
57
8va

# WHAT CHILD IS THIS?

Traditional English Melody
*Arranged by* FRED BOCK
*Adapted by* LLOYD LARSON

17
21
25
Warmly
f
30
35

39
Ped.
44
Ped.
49
53
58
Slowing
mp
mf
mp
p
pp

# ANGELS WE HAVE HEARD ON HIGH

FRENCH CAROL
*Arranged by* FRED BOCK
*Adapted by* LLOYD LARSON

21
Stronger
mp
mf
simile
25
29
33
37
41

44
48
52
56
60

64
68
72
pp
76
f rit.
79
a tempo
gradual decresc.
pp
slowly
rolled

# SILENT NIGHT! HOLY NIGHT!

FRANZ GRÜBER
*Arranged by* FRED BOCK
*Adapted by* LLOYD LARSON

17
21
25
29
pp
33

37
pp
41
pp
mf
45
(pp)
49
(pp)
53

57
Strongly
61
f
65
mp
mf
69
mp slower
mf
73
mp
pp

# MARY, DID YOU KNOW?

MARK LOWRY and BUDDY GREEN
*Arranged by* FRED BOCK
*Adapted by* LLOYD LARSON

**Pensively, with great feeling** (♩ = ca. 72-76)

20
24
mp
28
mf
32
ten.
f
mf
ten.
mp
Ped.
ten.
36

40
mf
44
f
48
52
56
Rhythmic and driving
f
legato

60
Rhythmic
ff sub. p
64
15ma
f ff mp
Ped. 15mb
68
72
mf
76
f

80
mf
mp
mf
84
15ma
ff sub. p
f ff mp
Ped. 15mb
88
mf
92
ten.
p
ten.
96
8va
bring out mel.
cresc.
rit.
mf
f
mf
Ped.
Ped.

# JOY TO THE WORLD!

GEORGE F. HANDEL
*Arranged by* FRED BOCK
*Adapted by* LLOYD LARSON

15
accel. e cresc.
19
sub. p
a tempo
23
27
8vb
8vb
31
ff
ff
f

accented
smoothly
mf
f
ff
L.H.
R.H.
8vb

# WE THREE KINGS

JOHN H. HOPKINS, JR.
*Arranged by* FRED BOCK
*Adapted by* LLOYD LARSON

Slow, plodding tempo

20
25
30
35
p
mp
40
simile

45
50
55
60
pp
p
mp
65
mf

70
f
74
78
83
p dim. poco a poco
87
rit.
pp

# AWAY IN A MANGER MEDLEY

J. E. SPILMAN, JAMES R. MURRAY,
and JOHANNES BRAHMS
*Arranged by* FRED BOCK
*Adapted by* LLOYD LARSON

20
24
28
32
pp
mel. p
36
40
mf

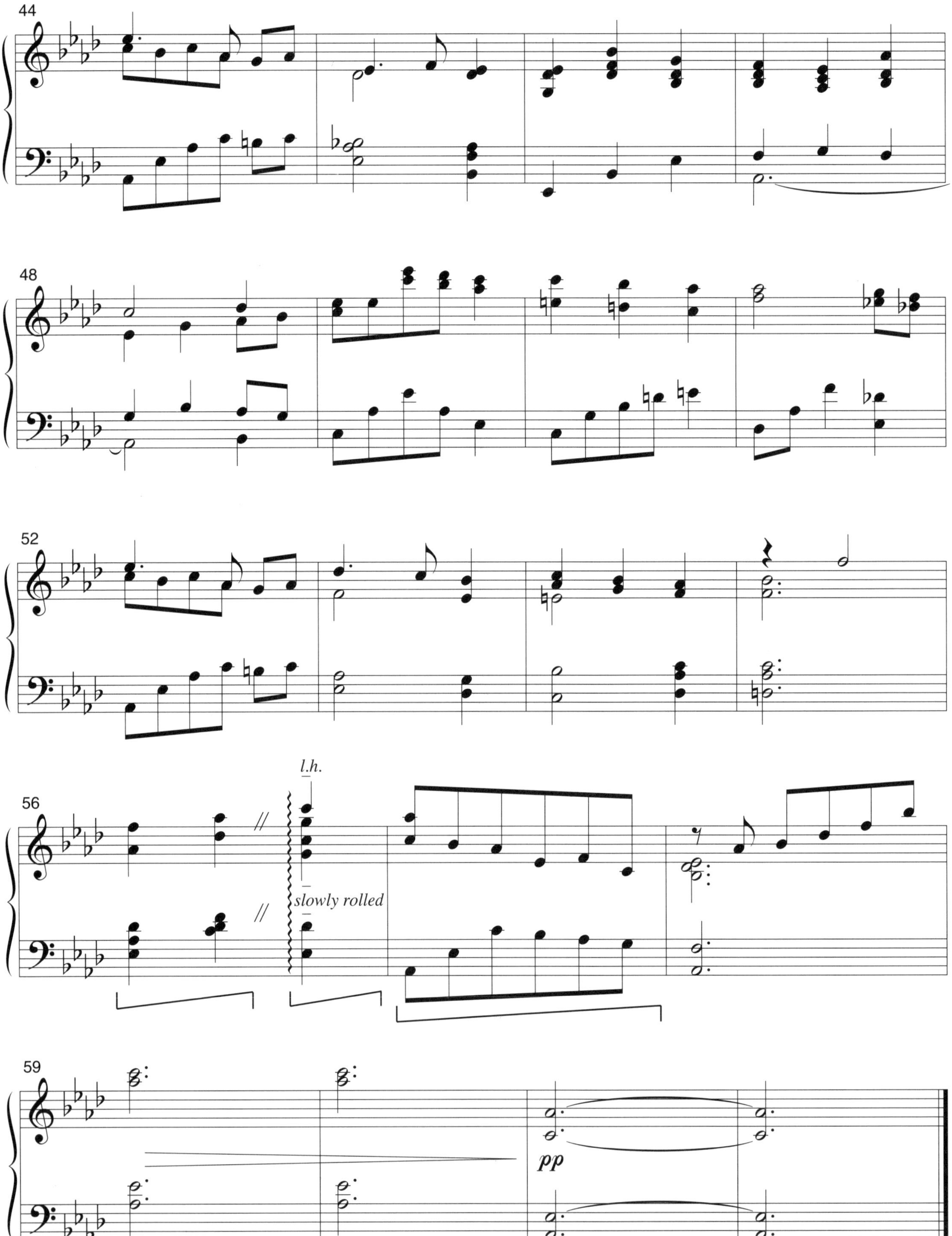
44
48
52
56
l.h.
slowly rolled
59
pp

# WE WISH YOU A MERRY CHRISTMAS

Traditional Carol
*Arranged by* FRED BOCK
*Adapted by* LLOYD LARSON

16
22
mf
26
29
32

35
38
f
41
45
f
49
ff
8va
fff

# THE LAST WORD

## Button Up Your Overcoat—

As I sit here writing this Christmas piano book foreword (I've finally learned the difference between *foreword* and *forward*!) the weather outside is frightful warm, about 92° and the lyric content of *Jingle Bells* and *Away In A Manger* are simply not cooling me down! What I really should do is pour ice water over myself, and start dreaming of a white Christmas. I'm trying to get into a wintry, Christmas mood, but it's not easy, this business of writing piano arrangements out of season!

I think I"ve found the answer, though, and that's to sit myself down and play through all twenty-five Christmas piano selections in this new book. I have always wanted to do an all-Christmas collection. In some of my other piano books I've snuck in a Christmas piece or two just to round it out, but now to have one complete source book of twenty-five—count 'em twenty-five—Christmas favorites everyone loves to play, is a dream fulfilled.

So, get yourself to a nice, in-tune piano, turn your calendar ahead to December, and play on. Here are a few of my favorite things: whiskers on kittens and my setting of THERE'S A SONG IN THE AIR. I must have been in a Chopin-esque mood that day, because this particular arrangement has many qualities of Chopin's piano etudes and nocturnes. Those chromatic lines need to be smoothly executed. "Practice makes perfect." (I didn't just make that up, but I'm 98% certain it's in the Bible somewhere), especially where there is a good deal of chromaticism involved. On the same day I wrote THERE'S A SONG IN THE AIR, I also wrote IT CAME UPON A MIDNIGHT CLEAR. I'm not sure which came first (I really should discipline myself to using opus numbers) but I'm sure you'll catch the similarities. And then there's JINGLE BELLS. I debated with myself whether or not to include this song in the book, but then decided a definite "yes!" "Jingle all the way," says I. My thinking was that it simply is not possible to get through the holidays without someone , somewhere, wanting to *play* or *hear* this song. JINGLE BELLS is like Mom, Apple Pie, and the 4th of the July, if you know what I mean. Now there are a few unusual notes and chords in this little number, so be careful little fingers what you play. I've made this list, and I've checked it twice, so *please* play the right notes on the chords in bars 3, 4, 5, 6, 7, and 8 of page 46. The notes are the same each time, only the octaves change. (See, I do try to make life easy for you piano players.) And, speaking of JINGLE BELLS, I did succumb to using the opening JINGLE BELLS motif a few times mingled amongst some of the other twenty-four carol arrangements. And just how many can you find? If you send me a letter clearly outlining page number, bar number, and score number where these excerpts can be found, and *if* you do find them *all,* I will send you a special gift. Send your cards and letters to me at Post Office Box 333, Tarzana, CA 91356-0333. This offer expires Christmas Eve.

If you are wanting to make some longer medleys out of these arrangements, feel free. Find the ones that fit together key-wise, and build a medley around a theme of your own. And don't forget about some of those other Fred Bock piano arrangements of Christmas tunes found in BOCK'S BEST #1 and #2.

With a happy Ho-Ho-Ho from sunny and warm Tarzana, California, I send forth these Christmas piano arrangements with lots of love. As you know, I actually *enjoy* writing piano arrangements, and from what I hear, many of you enjoy playing what I write. I hope this new book brings you happiness all year long, especially at Christmas, and even in June, September, or March.

Merry Christmas to all, and to all a good night.

FRED BOCK
Los Angeles, California

June 1984
(*Reprinted from Bock's Best #3*)